practical decision making

ian moore

**practical decision making
by ian moore**

Copyright © 2010 by Ian Moore
This material is the sole copyright of Ian Moore (2010). No part of this material may be reproduced in any form or by any means, electronic or mechanical, including photocopying, recording, or information recording and retrieval systems, for any purpose other than the purchaser's personal use, or translated into any language, without the express permission of the author. All rights reserved.
All trademarked products and company names used in this book are the property of their respective trademark holders.

ISBN: 978-1-4477-5112-0

about the author

Ian Moore has been involved with decision making, well all his life!

In his management roles logical decision making was essential. Later on in his consultancy roles he always believed that his role was to improve his client's decision making. He has approached decision making from many different angles. Having used logical decision making techniques for many years he became fascinated in how we limit our thinking. Running keynote presentations, writing books and running workshops in the areas of idea generation, innovation and spotting opportunities were all ways of broadening the ideas upon which people make their decisions. More recently he has become fascinated with how the mechanisms that have evolved in our brains actually make bad decisions more likely. His main current focus is giving keynote presentations and running workshops on how, by understanding the way that our brains limit our decision making ability, we can develop techniques to improve it.

He has published a number of books: 'Unpossible Ideas', 'Spotting Business Opportunities' and 'Unpossible Thinking' and is currently working on a book about how our brains have evolved to make poor business decisions.

His formal qualifications include a B.Sc.(Hons.) in Mathematics and Physics, an M.Sc. in Information Technology and an M.Sc. In Cognitive Neuroscience.

More importantly his informal qualifications include being a father, being a creative entrepreneur, believing that anything is possible and having a fascination about how our brains work.

His website is:

http://www.unthinkablethinking.com

table of contents

practical decision making	3
introduction	7
in a nutshell	11
what stops us making a decision?	12
intuitive decision making	15
pros and cons	18
pmi	24
swot	27
pest	31
pareto analysis	35
decision trees	38
force field analysis	44
cost benefit analysis	48
putting it all together	52
group decision making	54
getting buy in to decisions	57
common questions	59
want to know more	61

practical decision making

quote

"Making no decision is often the biggest failure."

Ian Livingston (Chief Executive of BT)

overview

Do we make logical decisions? The answer is usually no! They are often flavoured by our emotions, intuition, past experience and political agendas. Often fear of making a poor decision prevents us from making any decision at all. Too much information may prevent us from being able to work out the best option.

The techniques described here will help.

Becoming familiar with the techniques and practising them on a regular basis will dramatically improve your logical decision making ability.

introduction

what is decision making?

Decision making is a logical, intuitive and emotional exercise. All these components are necessary for humans to make decisions but it is often desirable to reduce the emotional and intuitive components. Here we concentrate very much on logical decision making rather than the other elements. I do not claim that this is the correct approach only that improving our logical decision making skills will make a significant difference to our personal and business lives.

Deciding **not** to make a decision **is** a decision! We may often do this because of lack of information, too many options, unclear or dangerous outcomes etc. All these, and more, if logically assessed, are valid reasons for not making a decision.

Prevaricating without any reason is **not** making a decision!

The techniques described here will help you **make** a decision, even if it is to not make a decision.

strengths and weaknesses

A favourite concept that I use regularly is that "all strengths are weaknesses and all weaknesses are strengths". For instance if you are good at talking that is a strength, but it may have a corresponding weakness, perhaps you are not as good as you could be at listening. On the other hand if you have a weakness such as having a tendency to get lost a lot then you will develop techniques to help you find your way, which people who do not get lost often would never develop. People who know me might know who I am talking about here :-)

I think this is a very useful concept to consider when you are using the logical decision making techniques discussed here and I will refer to this concept in a number of situations.

what is not covered here

The focus here is on logical decision making. I do not look at 'futures thinking', 'idea generation techniques' or 'problem solving approaches'. All of these can be used incredibly usefully in making better decisions, but they are covered elsewhere. Neither do I cover any of the aspects of how our brains work that bias us towards making bad decisions (although this is a strong interest on mine). My reasoning being: first learn how to make better logical decisions; then we can consider why this is not enough.

how much do bad decisions cost?

It is worth reflecting for a moment on how much bad decisions actually cost.

In business environments one major bad decision can cost huge amounts of money. Less noticeable are the many less major bad decisions that are made in an organisation on a daily basis that probably amount to much more.

The effects of bad decisions can be difficult to quantify but in your organisation:

- How many bad decisions are made?
- How much do they cost the organisation
    - on a daily basis?
    - annually?
- If you could make a small improvement in decision making how much would you save or make?

Hopefully this gives you some idea why good decision making needs to be addressed and focused on. In many organisations decisions and their effects might be focused on, but the actual process of making decisions is often ignored.

the importance of good decision making

But it is about more than just the cost!

If people are unconfident about their decision making they will either not make a decision (lost opportunity) or make the decision and then worry about it (increased stress). Even worse is when we don't make a decision **and** worry about it. Knowing that you have made the best possible decision helps to dramatically improve both of these. People who are confident that their decision making is based on sound principles will not only make fewer bad decisions (they will still make some) but will feel comfortable that they have made the best decision possible at that time.

in a nutshell

how to use these techniques

- Read the description of one technique
- Practise a simple form of the technique in a variety of situations
- Practise the more advanced forms of the technique (if there are any)
- Repeat for another technique
- When you have covered all the techniques try using them in combination

techniques covered here

- Intuitive decision making
- Pros and Cons
- PMI
- SWOT
- PEST
- Pareto analysis
- Decision trees
- Force field analysis
- Cost benefit analysis

what stops us making a decision?

You make a decision when you 'make up your mind'. The down side of this is that when you make a decision you have to let go of other ideas, options and possibilities. Some people find this difficult to do. There are many reasons for this including:

- Not having good decision making techniques
- Lack of confidence, not trusting yourself
- Lack of information
- Too much information to keep in your head at one time
- Disagreement between group members
- Trying to decide a big thing that could, and probably should, be split into smaller decisions
- Level of responsibility. If your decision affects others and carries consequences you may be reluctant to finalise things
- Fear of getting the decision wrong or making a mistake
- Avoiding closure on something because the next step after a decision is into the unknown
- Being emotionally attached to a certain outcome which is not the logical choice
- The opportunity cost of making a decision and thus letting go of other options
- Conflict with our personal values or priorities
- Social or organisational constraints
- Not wanting to create winners and losers
- Uncertainty over the consequences, especially if they seem to lead to a lose-lose situation

All of these problems will be helped significantly by practising and using the techniques described here.

Sometimes we prevaricate over the smallest decisions without knowing why. This may be caused by other things that are happening in our lives. It may be because we have no deadline for the decision and are spending too much time on the details. Some people naturally take more time in making a decision than others, this is not necessarily a bad thing but can have consequences if time is critical.

In order to make a decision we need some personal benefit for making it. One major benefit of making a decision is that you no longer need to expend mental energy on it, it is a 'weight off your mind". You can move on to other things and remove the stress and internal conflict that not making the decision causes.

To motivate ourselves to make a decision we need to focus on how we will feel after making the decision. What will be the benefits of making the decision? What good things will flow from the decision? In this way we can dispel the fear of making the decision. In the end it all comes down to the fear of consequences, this produces anxiety, which in turn fuels the fear. It is a downward spiral for many people. To drive out the consequences, look at any decision from these four perspectives:

1. What would happen if I did?
2. What would happen if I did not?
3. What would not happen if I did?
4. What would not happen if I did not?

Each of these is a subtly different question and you will get great clarity of the consequences of a decision by really thinking about them.

intuitive decision making

quote

"Trust your gut"

Barbara Walters

The human brain can process huge amounts of information unconsciously without it ever rising into consciousness. This is why intuitive decision making can be extremely powerful and should not be underestimated.

The problem with intuitive decision making is that it can seldom be quantified and so analysed. In groups 'group think' can be extremely pervasive and a group's intuitive decision making should be taken with extreme caution. Also intuitive decision making can just be plain wrong! In many situations the human brain is very poor at spotting 'differences' whilst being much better at spotting 'similarities'. For this reason, if something has always happened a certain way in the past, we are much more likely to assume it will happen the same way again, which may well not be the case because we have not noticed what has changed.

So should we use intuitive decision making or not? It can be very powerful in some cases and totally incorrect in others. There is no easy answer.

(For more information on intuitive decision making see 'Blink' by Malcolm Gladwell.)

People have different ways of accessing their intuition and

"knowing" when they have made a good decision. On a personal level there may be a number of factors involved, possibly just outside of your awareness, that let you know when a decision is right for you. Think about a time where you made a decision that you were happy with. With that decision in mind, consider the following summary statements and notice which resonates with you or makes sense:

- You felt good about the decision and just knew it was the right thing.
- The decision made sense and it just seemed like the logical choice or sensible thing to do. It ticked all the boxes or you were happy that you could cross the I's and dot the T's.
- You looked at all the options, you could see how it would work or you considered the various perspectives and it appeared to be the best option.
- You spoke to some people, had discussion around the various options, it sounded like a good approach.

Knowing which of the above works for you will help you evaluate whether your intuitive decision making is working well, or whether you have not really nailed the decision down just yet.

You can also think of times in the past when, in hindsight, you made a bad decision and notice how that seemed to you. If you get the same feeling again it could mean that your intuitive decision making is off track.

tip

Flip a coin. As it is in the air, think of which way up you hope it will land. Let the coin fall to the floor and don't look at it. You have your answer! If you get nothing while the coin is in the air catch it and look at the coin. Does what the answer the coin gives you fill you with relief or dread? You now have a direct communication from your intuitive self and you have your answer. The coin is just a trigger to get you in touch with your intuition. Practise this and then you won't need the coin.

pros and cons

quote

"Planning is an unnatural process: it is much more fun to do something. The nicest thing about not planning is that failure comes as a complete surprise rather than being preceded by a period of worry and depression."

Sir John Harvey-Jones

This is the simplest and probably the best known way of making decisions but may well be the only way you need, especially with some of the extensions that you can use with it.

To use this method you simply draw a table and list all the positive and negatives effects of making the decision:

Pros	Cons
( )	( )
( )	( )
( )	( )
( )	
( )	

tip

> You might want to leave this table on your desk for a few hours or overnight to let your subconscious work on it and spot more 'pros' and 'cons'.

The simplest way of using this is to make your decision based on the total numbers of items in each column. If there are more 'pros' than 'cons' then make the decisions, if not, don't.

In reality, however, many people still feel unhappy with the outcome and feel as if something is holding them back from taking the appropriate action. Even though the 'pros' significantly outweigh the 'cons' you might still feel hesitant about taking the decision. If the 'cons' outweigh the 'pros' you might still feel that this is the correct decision to make (see 'Intuitive Decision Making'). This may be because some of the items have more weight in your mind than others or that there might be some hidden 'pros' and 'cons' which have not risen to your conscious mind as yet.

weighting items

So, firstly, we could try to put some weights on each item. We can go through the lists and assign to each item a 'significance value' of between 1 and 10, where 1 is not very significant and 10 is highly significant. By adding up the items in each column you may get a better analysis of the decision.

strengths and weaknesses

Secondly we can try to extend the number of items in each list. If we assume that 'all strengths are weaknesses, and all weaknesses are strengths' we can take each item in the 'pros' column and map it to three items in the 'cons' column. For example, if I am thinking about buying a new car:

Pros	Cons
(Will look new)	

we might map this to a number of 'cons':

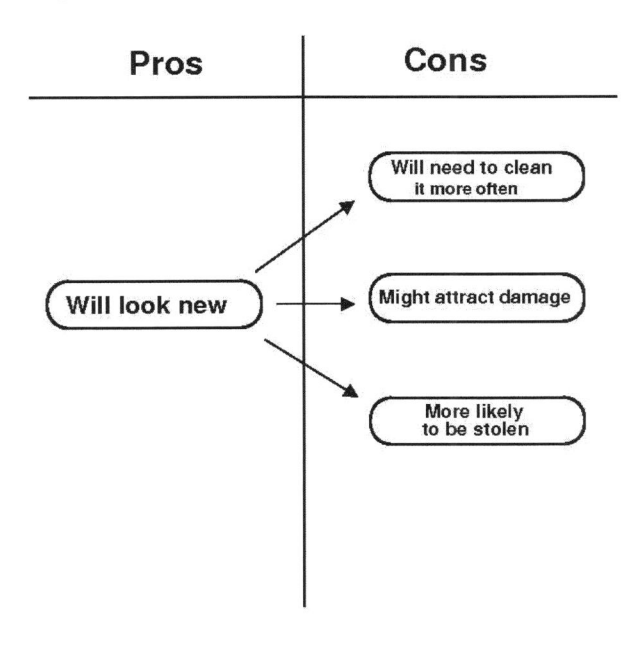

Pros	Cons
(Will look new)	(Will need to clean it more often)
	(Might attract damage)
	(More likely to be stolen)

15

So now for that single 'pro' we have three new 'cons'. (Don't worry if some of the new 'cons' were already on the list.). We can now repeat this for the rest of the 'pros'. Similarly we can look at the list of 'cons' and map each of these to three 'pros'.

tip

> You can choose to do more than three items for each mapping and, all although this is sometimes useful, it may become a bit complex. If you do want to do more a large free space and post-it notes may help.

tip

> You can also dig deeper with your analysis . If you map a 'pro' to three 'cons' then take each of the three 'cons' and map them back again to three more 'pros' then you will potentially have nine new 'pros'. This can be useful for a deeper analysis but can get complex. Use your judgement.

making your decision

Now if we look through the lists we might find that the balance has changed and you may have a much deeper insight into the ramifications of the decision. You can delete the duplicates in each column but the very fact that there are duplicates may suggest that this factor is very important for you.

pmi

quote

> "Thus the task is not so much to see what no one yet has seen, but to think what nobody has yet thought about that which everybody sees."
>
> Schopenhauer

This technique is called 'Plus / Minus / Interesting' and can be thought of as an extension to the 'pros and cons' technique but with another column for 'Interesting'. We generally classify situations into "good" and "bad". This leaves us nowhere to identify things which are neither of these things. These could lead to new thinking. To satisfy our conventional thinking it is beneficial to classify the "good" and "bad" so that we can then can move on to thinking about the "interesting". This "interesting" category can contain ideas that just come to mind whilst you are thinking up the "good" and the "bad". You can also generate ideas for the "interesting" by looking at the "good" ideas and seeing if any of these ideas generate "interesting" ideas. The "bad" ideas can also be used in a similar way by using an "if this was not the case" provocation. The "interesting" ideas should not be evaluated but simply written down. Leave your evaluating for the "good" and the "bad".

The technique is an interesting way of combining your logical and creative thinking in a positive and productive way.

using the technique

- On a piece of paper draw three columns with the words "Plus", "Minus" and "Interesting" at the top.

- For the decision you are trying to make, write down words or phrases as they occur to you in the relevant columns.

- If you are starting to feel stuck, stop, look at the "pluses" and see what "interesting" ideas these generate. Also look at the "minuses" and see what "interesting" ideas are generated. You may also like to try considering some interesting ideas and see if any new interesting ideas are generated.

strengths and weaknesses

We can extend this technique in similar ways that we extended the 'pros' and 'cons' technique. If we assume that 'all strengths are weaknesses, and all weaknesses are strengths' we can take each item in the 'pros' column and map it to three items in the 'cons' column and some items in the 'interesting' column. We can then do the same with the 'cons' and 'interesting' columns.

making your decision

You can evaluate your decision in the same way that you evaluated the results of the 'pros' and 'cons' technique, however the biggest strength of this technique is the fact that you have generated a number of items in the 'interesting' column. These may well give you some really good indications on the best decision to make.

swot

quote

"If a man will begin with certainties he shall end his doubts; but if he will be content to begin with doubts he shall end in certainties."

Francis Bacon

This technique originated in marketing but can be used in any area of decision making.

Four factors are taken into consideration:

- **S**trengths: What are the strengths of the decision?
- **W**eaknesses: What are the weaknesses?
- **O**pportunities: What opportunities could exist if the decision is made?
- **T**hreats: What threats would exist if the decision is made?

Strengths and Weaknesses are **internal** factors

Opportunities and Threats are **external** factors

Strengths and Opportunities are **helpful** factors

Weaknesses and Threats are **unhelpful** factors

using the technique

Firstly you should define the objective of the decision. e.g. 'the objective is to generate more sales'. It is important to identify the objective clearly before starting the swot analysis and stick with that during the analysis. For instance 'generating more sales' may not 'generate more profit'. If you have decided that the first objective is the one you want to work with then stick with that during the analysis. You can always do other swots with other objectives, in fact it is often very useful to do a swot for a number of related objectives.

The usual way of running a swot analysis is to draw a square of 2*2 boxes on a piece of paper and write down ideas in each box:

Strengths	Weaknesses
Opportunities	Threats

tip

> For complex situations or group decision making you can use a large wall or desk space and post-it notes.

extending the external factors

The external factors in a swot are the 'opportunities' and 'threats' boxes. You can increase the number of items in each of these boxes by doing a **pest** analysis on them.

strengths and weaknesses

As with the other techniques for decision making you can apply the idea that 'all strengths are weaknesses and all weaknesses are strengths.
For example you can convert each strength to three weaknesses and each weakness to three strengths.

You can also convert each 'opportunity' to three 'threats' and each 'threat' to three opportunities.

It may also be possible to convert the 'internal' factors to 'external' factors and vice versa but you will probably find that these do not generate as many items.

making your decision

If the 'strengths' and 'opportunities' significantly outweigh the 'weaknesses' and 'threats' then it is likely that taking the decision will turn out to be a good one. If the opposite is true then it is likely that you should not make this decision or make an opposite one.

Remember if you don't get to any firm conclusion with this technique it is likely to be worthwhile for you to change your objective and run the swot analysis again.

pest

quote

"Complexity is the decadence of society; simplicity is the path of reality and salvation."

Egyptian Proverb

This technique helps to identify the effects and consequences of external factors on a decision. It looks at the following influences:

- **P**olitical
- **E**conomic
- **S**ocial
- **T**echnological

Political:

These are factors related to how much the government intervenes in the economy. Examples include taxation, employment law, international trade etc. You need to also consider political stability and the effects of a change of government in this influence.

Economic:

These are factors related to the economy including interest rates, inflation, employment levels etc.

Social:

Includes factors such as population growth, the age distribution of the population and socially acceptable and unacceptable behaviours.

Technological:

Includes technological trends, computerisation, automation etc.

using the technique

The simplest way to use this is to draw four boxes on a piece of paper and label them and then populate the boxes with as many effects and consequences of the decision that you can think of. The resulting lists will help with deciding whether the decision is a good one or not.

extending the model (pestel)

The model is commonly extended to include another two factors:

Environmental:

These are factors such as climate, climate change, weather etc.

Legal:

Factors related to legislation in a specific country of operation such as the law relating to discrimination, health and safely, employment etc.

extending the model further:

The model can be extended further to include Education and Demographics (the **steepled** model) or in fact in any other way that you might find useful. In most cases though a relatively simple four or six factor model is all that is needed. Adding further factors tends to cause some overlap between influences and can cause some confusion about which box to put an individual factor in.

making your decision

This technique can be used as a decision making technique in its own right. The usual way is to look at the output of the technique and decide on the individual factors that most affect your decision. Considering these will usually make the correct decision more obvious.

This technique can also be used in conjunction with a swot analysis, helping to populate the 'opportunities' and 'threats' boxes.

pareto analysis

quote

> Men stumble over the truth from time to time, but most pick themselves up and hurry off as if nothing had happened.
>
> Winston Churchill

This technique uses a variation of the Pareto principle i.e. "80% of the advantage comes from 20% of the work". In many situations changing 20% of the situation can resolve 80% of the problems. If we can identify a small number of changes we can make which will make a large difference then we can have a large impact with a small amount of effort.

This approach is particularly useful in innovation scenarios where a quick short term gain can produce and easy and early win and create buy in to the innovation process.

using the technique

- Create a list of the factors that may be responsible for causing your desired outcome.
- When you are reasonably sure that you have most of the significant factors listed create a second column with an approximate percentage estimate of each factor's contribution to the outcome.

- Starting with the largest percentage and working downwards from a percentage point of view create a running total of the percentages. When you have reached about 80% then stop. You have now identified the most significant factors.

caution

This technique does not always work. If you find that you have many factors all with relatively small significance percentages then most of the factors will need to be included to get to the 80% mark. In this case the Pareto analysis may be of little use to you. In cases where you have only a relatively small number of factors (about 20%) needed to make up the 80% significance, this is where this analysis is the most useful.

You should also be cautious of factors that grow over time, they can start of with a small significance but one which gets larger as time progresses.

tip

If you enter the factors and percentages in a spreadsheet it is very easy to sort the spreadsheet by the percentages column and create another column for cumulative percentages.

making your decision

Once you have established the 20% (or so) of the factors that have the most (80%) significance then you can implement those ignoring the others. This will hopefully give you the vast majority of the advantage of the decision with a small amount of effort.

You of course can run the analysis again after a period of time has elapsed. The Pareto principle should still apply. Of the original factors which are left you should find that 20% of these are responsible for 80% of the remaining issues. Of course because you have already implemented the 20% easiest parts of the decision running the next analysis will not produce as big a difference and will take more work but this is a good approach for a rolling implementation of a decision.

decision trees

quote

"If there are two courses of action,
you should take the third."
Jewish Proverb.

A decision tree is a visual tool for analysing decisions. In using it you generate a tree-like graph of decisions and their consequences. In the simplest form of this technique:

Squares: represent decisions

Triangles: represent end points

When the graph is completed you can then add probabilities for each of the individual branches and from the the overall probabilities of the end points.

using the technique

As a simple example let's suppose that I decide that I want to travel from my home to a hotel in town A. So let's draw the options in a decision tree:

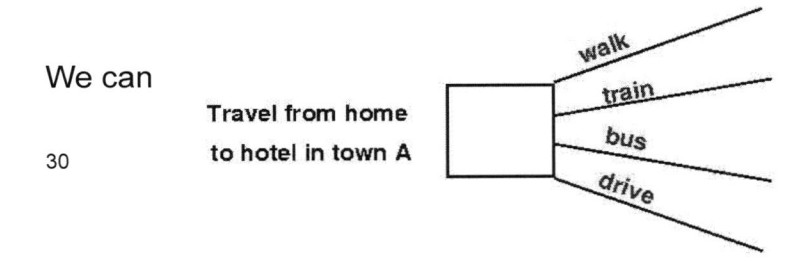

We can

Travel from home
to hotel in town A

- walk
- train
- bus
- drive

now add some %'s to reflect either our preferences or an estimate of some factor that we would like to consider (e.g. cost, estimated likelihood, etc.). In this case I will use personal preferences:

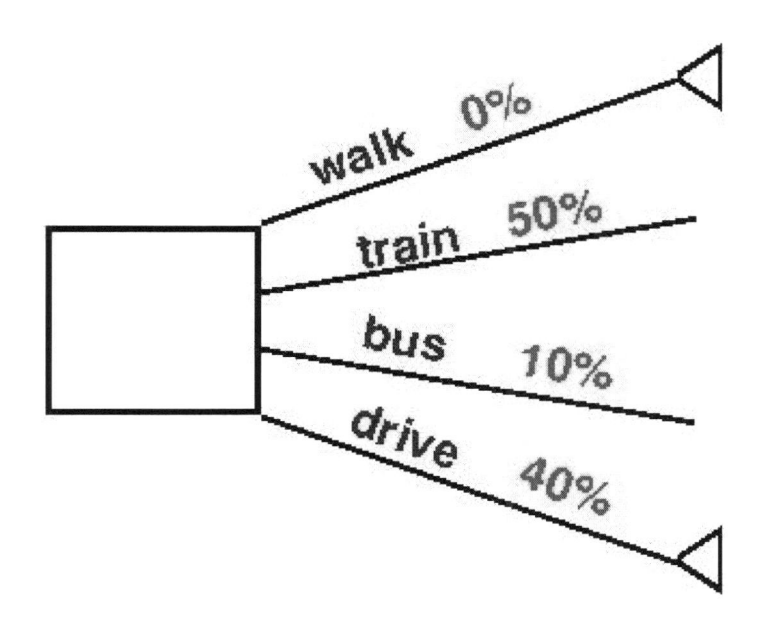

```
         walk   0%
              ◁
         train  50%
              ―――
         bus    10%
         drive  40%
              ◁
```

I am assuming here that the train station is close to my home. For 'walk' I have added 0% because it is a long distance to town A. The bus takes a long time but it is quite cheap so I have given it 10%.

Notice that I have also added end points to 'walk' and 'drive' as they both get me to my destination. 'Train' and 'bus' however do not get me to my final destination so I now extend my decision tree by adding more decision points, options and estimates:

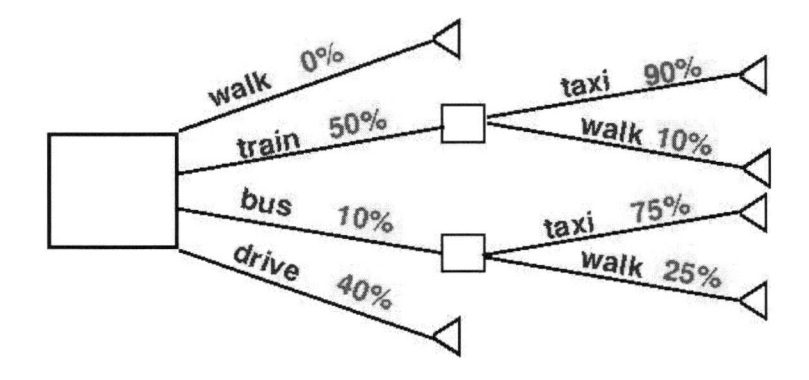

We can now multiply the %'s and see what the final end point %'s are:

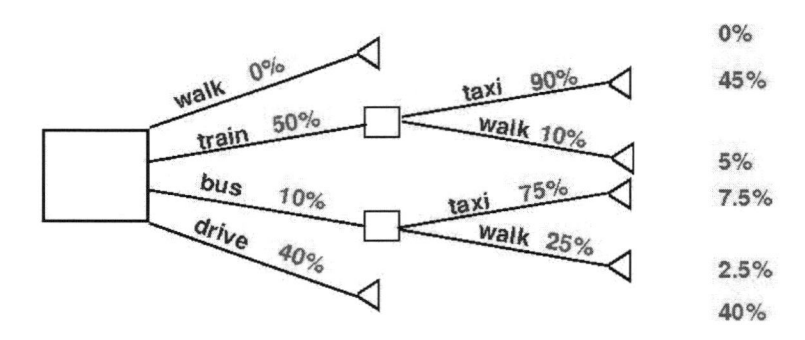

So our conclusion should be that we should take the train and a taxi (45%).

extending the %'s

In this example I have used personal preferences only. You

could also do this based on cost (or any other factor) simply use another colour for another % on each branch.

caution

This is a very simple example but even here I have simplified the decision tree. I have not considered for instance how I would get from my home to the train station. Decision trees can rapidly become very complex, indeed this is one of their strengths as they allow us to consider options that we might normally ignore. Try using a large wall space covered with flip chart paper (or a large white board) for your decision trees.

tip

Before starting your decision tree decide on the level of detail you wish to consider and the number of %'s you want to take into account. For example it can get very complicated if you use more that two types of %'s. When you have decided on the level of detail that you require try to stick to this, don't be dragged off into too much detail. In fact deciding the detail you should go down to in each decision tree that you do is one of the skills that you will develop by using them. In some cases a very high degree of detail is needed, in others all but the major option branches can be ignored.

adding chance events

You can make your decision trees even more elaborate by adding:

    Circles: Chance events

For example:

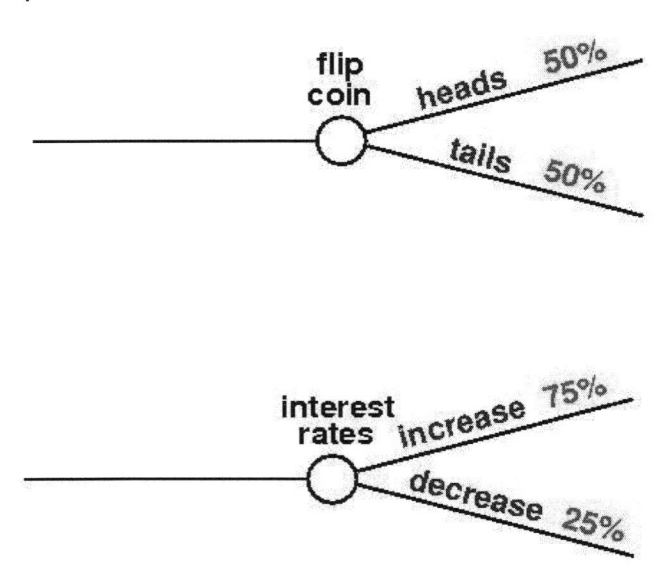

```
                    flip      heads   50%
                    coin    ╱
         ───────────○
                         ╲   tails   50%
```

```
                  interest            75%
                   rates   increase
         ───────────○
                         ╲  decrease   25%
```

making your decision

The %'s at the end points should be all that you need to make a decision. If you feel that this is the wrong decision you should consider:

- whether the %'s you have allocated are correct

- whether the level of detail in the branches is too high or too low
- whether you are using the correct estimate (e.g. your %'s may be 'increased sales' when they should be 'increased profits')

force field analysis

quote

"I have noticed even people who claim everything is predestined, and that we can do nothing to change it, look before they cross the road."

Professor Stephen Hawking

This is a framework for looking at the forces that influence a decision. There are two types of forces:
- **Helping** forces: Drive movement towards the decision
- **Hindering** forces: Resist movement towards the decision

using the technique

The first step is to draw a box within which you write the decision. Then you list all the helping and hindering forces. The example I will use here is whether I should buy a new car:

```
helping forces          decision          hindering forces

    reliability    →                  ←    cost
                       buy
                        a
 decreased         →   new
 maintenance
                       car        ←    time
    look new    →       ?

                                  ←    which model ?
   fuel economy   →
```

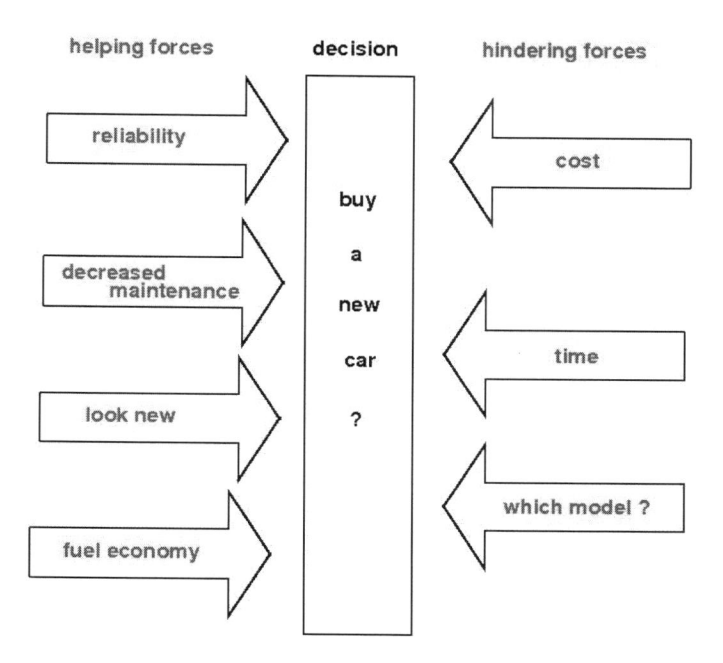

Having spent some time trying to think of all the forces in play you then assign a strength to each force between 1 and 5 where 1 is weak and 5 is strong:

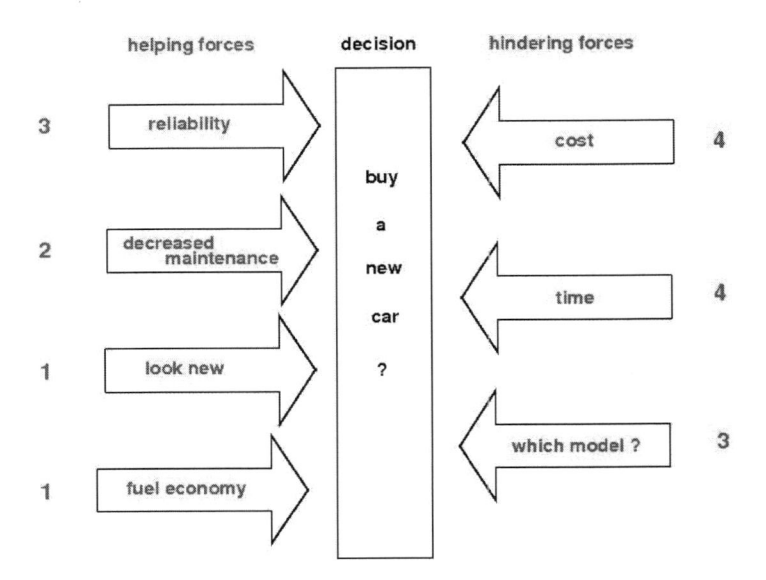

helping forces		decision		hindering forces	
3	reliability		cost	4
2	decreased maintenance	buy a new car ?	time	4
1	look new		which model ?	3
1	fuel economy			

We can then add up the strengths of the forces to give a helping:hindering ratio. In this case it is 7:11 so initially it looks like the decision to buy a new car will not be made because the hindering forces outweigh the helping forces.

tip

> The forces in a force field analysis are dynamic and will change over time. Doing the same analysis in a months or a years time will usually produce a different result.

If we do want the decision to go ahead we can now look for ways to increase the helping forces and decrease the hindering forces.

Looking at the hindering forces:

Cost: If I leased a car then I could change this from 4 to 2.
Time: As I don't have much time to look at other models I could always just buy the same model which would change this score from 4 to 1.
Which model: Would therefore also decrease from 3 to 1.

So by decreasing the hindering forces the analysis now gives 7:4, much more promising.

In my example the helping forces will mostly increase with time as reliability, decreased maintenance and fuel economy become more significant. We might say that in a few months time that these will change to 4, 3 and 3 respectively. (It is unlikely in a few months time that I will care any more about my car looking new, so that score would stay the same.) So in a few months time this may change to 11:4, even more promising.

My conclusion from this analysis is therefore that I should lease the same model of car as I have already either now or in a few months time.

cost benefit analysis

quote

"What ails the truth is that it is mainly uncomfortable, and often dull. The human mind seeks something more amusing, and more caressing."

H.L. Mencken

at it's simplest

A very basic cost benefit analysis simply lists all the costs associated with a decision and all the benefits (in monetary terms). If the costs outweigh the benefits then don't do it. If the benefits outweigh the costs then do it.

Of course in real life the issues are:

- listing all the costs and benefits
- assigning accurate monetary values to them

caution

Most research into the effectiveness of cost benefit analyses suggests that people consistently underestimate the costs and overestimate the benefits.

dealing with time

Costs and benefits over the period that it takes to implement a decision need to be converted into some common form so that they are comparable. Usually this is 'current value'.

In a simple example, if it costs us £1 million to implement a decision and in one year's time we expect a benefit of £1.1 million, we cannot say that the benefit is £0.1 million. We need to convert the £1.1 million in a year's time into the equivalent in today's terms. At the very least we need to take into account the rate of inflation for the year and reduce the value of the £1.1 million appropriately.

In complex decisions where many costs and benefits will occur over the time period this is by no means a trivial task and also requires accurate estimation of the factors which will affect the costs and benefits.

opportunity cost

If you didn't spend the £1 million what other opportunities might there be?

At the simplest you need to consider how much the £1 million would grow if invested. In six months time might we need this money for another decision that we may not even have thought of yet? Other already planned decisions may be adversely affected by this decision, what would be our losses if these other decisions are not implemented?

risk

We need to be able to factor risk in as well. As we all know not all decisions that we make actually work out. Can we estimate the percentage likelihoods of success and failure at each point in the implementation and adjust the costs and benefits appropriately?

A decision might not be a complete failure. Can we estimate the benefits from a partial success and the likelihood of this happening?

not just money

A good cost benefit analysis will take into account factors other than money, which will tend to be even harder to quantify. For example a failure could result in a loss of reputation, how much is that worth and can it be quantified|? At the very least an educated guess should be included for this. Will a success be copied by competitors?

learning

When doing cost benefit analyses it is important to put mechanisms in place that will capture inaccuracies in your predications. These can then be learnt from and fed into future analyses. Some events will be unpredictable but most will have some element of predictability in them and capturing this information will be invaluable to future analyses. Some key issues to be aware of are:

- an over reliance of similar past projects
- overestimating benefits
- underestimating costs
- overly enthusiastic staff

running an analysis

In summary:

- list all benefits and costs
- include opportunity costs
- include risk factors
- include less tangible aspects of success and failure
- implement a review mechanism for improving future analyses
- assign a value to each element considered
- convert all values to 'current values'

If after all this your analysis suggests that the benefits outweigh the costs then take the decision, if not then don't.

putting it all together

quote

"It ain't so much the things we don't know that get us into trouble. It's the things that we know that just ain't so."

Artemis Ward

We have covered a number of analytical decision making techniques. There are others but mastering these techniques should be sufficient for improving your logical decision making.

To improve even further:

- practise each technique in a variety of situations and add your own improvements and style to them
- start combining techniques (this is probably best done when you have mastered each individual technique)

choosing a technique

As you practise the techniques you will find that some work better in some situations than others. In other situations other techniques will work better. With experience try to identify the technique that works best in a particular situation and use that technique.

For example you might find that SWOT analyses work well for

you. That is great, but don't forget to try other techniques as well.

combining techniques

Remember that "all strengths are weaknesses and all weaknesses are strengths". When you become comfortable with a technique there are real opportunities in trying others in combination with it. For example if SWOT works well for you try using the 'pros and cons' technique to elaborate on the items in your SWOT table. Try using PEST to add different perspectives to your SWOT.

If you are used to using cost benefit analyses try using decision trees to improve the percentage likelihoods of outcomes. Try using PMI to add 'interesting' elements to your analyses.

Each technique will improve your decision making. Once you are used to using all the techniques, combining them will improve your decision making dramatically.

group decision making

quote

"Never use one head when two will do."

Anon.

Each of the techniques described can be used effectively by yourself but can also be used in groups. A group adds a lot of richness to the techniques but the different opinions can make agreement more difficult. The following approaches work well for gaining consensus within a group.

populating your analysis

One of the great strengths of group decision making is the variety of perspectives and the richness this gives when populating your decision making techniques with ideas. For instance in a SWOT analysis you can get the whole group to do this very effectively and quickly, producing much more comprehensive ideas that an individual would.

tip

> Rather than having people standing around discussing the ideas that go into the analysis, give them each a pad of post-its. Ask them to write down as many ideas as they can in five minutes (one idea per post-it). When they have finished put them all up on a wall and get the whole group to organise them into themes. Then give each theme a name. This name then goes into the analysis.

weights

In techniques such as 'decision trees' different people may disagree about the percentages that should be assigned to each option. This can lead to a very useful debate but at some point people need to be able to agree to differ. One way of coming to a compromise is to allocate "error %'s" to the %'s. For example if Joe thinks that the % should be 75% and Mary thinks it should be 25% then you can settle on 50% +/- 25%.

When doing the analysis you can use both ends of the %'s to produce a range for the decision making technique e.g. use all the lowest %'s to create a final 'worst case' figure and all the highest %'s to create a final 'best case' figure. This will give you a feel for the variation in the decision making process.

voting

Another way to resolve differences is to allocate votes. For example give everyone 10 votes which they can allocate in any way they want. One person might want to allocate all their 10 votes to one outcome, another may want to spread their votes across different outcomes, it is up to them. When everyone has voted the votes are totalled and the winner is the decision that is adopted.

Note: the boss gets the same number of votes as everyone else!

emotions

Now that a decision has been made it is important to get feedback on people's feelings. This is often ignored in business environments. For example in a recruitment interview one candidate might come out as 'perfect' by all the criteria set before the interview. However if no one likes the person they are unlikely to work well in the team. It is important to get feedback about people's feelings about a decision.

agreeing an action plan

And finally after coming to a group decision it is critical to agree a group action plan which everyone buys into. What happens next, who does what by when, etc.

getting buy in to decisions

So now you have made your decision and are about to implement it. All seems clear to you and the implementation should be fairly straightforward. But have you asked all the people who will be affected and got their buy in? Surprisingly this stage is often overlooked when implementing a decision and can lead to disastrous consequences.

identifying stakeholders

A stakeholder is a person who will be affected in any way but your decision. They are not necessarily always just the obvious people. Think about who will be affected, these may include:

- Your staff
- Your boss
- Your CEO and board
- Other groups within your organisation
- The customer
- The public
- The press
-
-

Try to identify as many groups of people as possible and then …..

establishing stakeholder needs

….. go and find out what they think!

Of course this may not always be possible but having identified all the stakeholders this will at least give you some feel for where the main issues might arise.

Quite often stakeholder needs may be very simple and easily satisfied by incorporating them into your decision. If this is not the case then you need to be able to get them on board. If this is not possible you may need to go back to your decision making process and think again or be prepared for the consequences and push ahead regardless.

common questions

What is the best technique to use?

> The answer of course is that it depends! Some techniques, such as SWOT, are naturally more aligned with product and service development but it can be used in many other situations with excellent results. Similarly other techniques not associated with products and services may help in this area. Other techniques apply naturally to other situations but all techniques should have value for any type of decision making.

Should I use only one technique?

> Yes and no!
> I would suggest using only one technique until you have become comfortable with it. Then do the same with each of the other techniques in turn. When you have become comfortable will all the techniques try using some of them together.

I have too much information, how do I make a decision?

> I think that the answer to this is to methodically use the techniques described. You may need to practise a technique first on simpler decisions but when you have become comfortable with the technique you will be able to apply it to more complex situations.

I am under pressure to make a decision, what do I do?

> Applying the techniques in a non-pressured

environment will help. Get yourself away from the office and distracting interruptions if possible and concentrate on applying the techniques in a cool, calm and collected manner.

Is logical decision making all there is?

> I personally think not. Our brains have evolved over hundreds of thousands of years for survival purposes and we have developed some very hard wired thinking and decision making processes. I firmly believe that an understanding of these built in processes can dramatically improve our decision making. But improving our logical decision making is a very good place to start.